# GUIDANCE *from* THE GOD *of* SEAHORSES

# GUIDANCE *from* THE GOD *of* SEAHORSES

*poems*

KEATS CONLEY

GREEN WRITERS PRESS *Brattleboro, Vermont*

Printed in the United States

10 9 8 7 6 5 4 3 2

Green Writers Press is a Vermont-based publisher whose mission is to spread a message of hope and renewal through the words and images we publish. Throughout, we will adhere to our commitment to preserving and protecting the natural resources of the earth. To that end, a percentage of our proceeds will be donated to environmental activist groups. Green Writers Press gratefully acknowledges support from individual donors, friends, and readers to help support the environment and our publishing initiative.

*Giving Voice to Writers & Artists Who Will Make the World a Better Place*
Green Writers Press | Brattleboro, Vermont
www.greenwriterspress.com

ISBN: 978-1-9505849-9-4

COVER PHOTO: JUSTIN HOFMAN
Used with permission.

Printed on recycled paper by Bookmobile.
Based in Minneapolis, Minnesota, Bookmobile began as a design and typesetting production house in 1982 and started offering print services in 1996.
Bookmobile is run on 100% wind- and solar-powered clean energy.

# Contents

*For my mother, Diane Raptosh*

"... every species of animal and plant now living [are] the individual letters which go to make up one of the volumes of our earth's history; and, as a few lost letters may make a sentence unintelligible, so the extinction of the numerous forms of life which the progress of cultivation invariably entails will necessarily render obscure this invaluable record of the past."

—Alfred Russel Wallace

Wallace, A. R. (1962). *The Malay Archipelago: the land of the orang-utan and the bird of paradise; a narrative of travel, with studies of man and nature.* Courier Corporation.

# GUIDANCE

*from*

# THE GOD

*of*

# SEAHORSES

# The God of Coyotes

In the beginning all was water and space like a hollow shell. I crafted you from the shadow of a cumulus cloud, straying over open plains. My companion; a hero and an antihero. I let you scatter the stars and then name the loci: *Lupus, Vulpecula*, and *Ursa Minor*. Feast your eyes on the Milky Way. Remember to always relish a good persimmon. Spit the seeds into the sky and wink. Drink tea made of corn silk and shelter yourself in the husks. Don't mourn the waning moon. Without death, the seeds would never unpeel themselves.

# The God of Horseshoe Crabs

I felt the need for nine eyes: two for mates, and the rest for moonlight. Two thousand photoreceptors demanded two-thousand titles: Snow Moon, Seed Moon, Egg Moon, Oak Moon, Sprouting Grass Moon. A moon and a month are cognates, like *shadow* and *shade, strange* and *extraneous*. They are the pooled blood of language. A month should be based on a Moon's movement relative to a star. A mouth should be based in the center of the legs, amid the flavors of salt, fish, and grit. Sprinkle your next generation, polish sand into emeralds until every grain is your own Green Moon.

# The God of Mosquitoes

Before you, evenings in the universe rolled in and receded. Time wrapped her infinite arms like a weighted blanket . . . Even Gods nod off at times. I pulled your wings from water to intrude upon silence like a violin. Instead, the sound waves converged on a sharper sinusoid. Ninety million more evenings, and it's nearly endearing . . . Which came first—the itch or the instinct to scratch? Let your sound echo the madness of what doesn't matter: straying eyebrows, edged lawns, ironed jeans . . . A good *swat*! jolts me back into omnipotence, skin welted by the insoluble practice of sleep.

# The God of Olms

Do not confuse an olm and a psalm. One is a human fish, the other a hymn. Psalm 148:7: *Praise the Lord from the earth, you dragons, and all deeps.* An olm is a cave dragon, distinct from an *om*—that sacred sound. Om and olms share a universe beyond the moon. A century slips past in a syllable. Olm, let your eyes regress in primordial darkness; let the world see through you. Breathe in through your lucent pink gills. Breathe out through the cathedral of your larval body.

## The God of Galápagos Tortoises

Your saddleback was the ashram for Darwin's first tree pose. I dare say antediluvian . . . maybe. Chronology evades me. . . . Somewhere behind my eyes lies this image of outstretched necks, bobbing like wine bottles over the sea. Lonesome George of the Pinta Island, now known for *Being an endling.* Try on this earworm for the Anthropocene: *I'd like to teach the world to sing, this endling's the real thing.* Does it tap the toes like *A little dab'll do ya?*

# The God of Daddy Long Legs

Every ten days, split your body and drag new legs from the casings.
After each meal, draw every leg to your mouth and floss your jaws.
Repurpose your legs as eyes, ears, nose and tongue. Move with
the grace of forget-me-nots—on the line between insect and seed,
tripping the light with an octagon of toes. Keep your nerves to the
ground and your thorax to the air. Samba down sidewalks. Breathe
through your tracheae. Swing dance like a sermon, like a quarter
note turning to a semibreve. Pitch toes-first to the wind. If your legs
detach, keep moving; keep bristling land with your broom feet for
another half-billion years.

## The God of Northern White Rhinos

Now it's just the two of you: mother and daughter enclosed with these
could-be southern surrogates, a million years divorced. You with a
higher head carriage, they with more prominent folds in their skin.
The last ambassadors of a subspecies, I watched your horns sawn off
by chainsaw, ground down to the growth plate. Saw, in my mind's eye,
the Statue of Liberty, holding nothing but an empty cup.

# The God of Pangolins

I genetically modified this body from a pine cone. Added a
tongue that, when extended, could stretch to the eyeballs. Tastes
like boba tea. Nine years running, the world celebrates the third
Saturday in February. Tweets into the firmament of the internet:
#WorldPangolinDay, #I<3pangolins! And this one: @Marvelous.
Creatures instagrams pangopup biscuits. Two teaspoons ground ginger
biting back on the tongue like words you wish could be withdrawn.
Maybe hope is not the thing with feathers but with scales, armored
and ready to unroll itself.e

## The God of Greater Sage-Grouse

Here in the sagebrush steppe is where I learned to breathe—here, in this landscape like a clear idea. Meditation isn't leaving your mind behind—it's rooting a thought thicket in an underground rhizome, ceding silver-blue limbs to vacant skies. Stop me if I'm preaching. Tilt back your head. Inflate the skin of your gular sacs. Devour the air and then set it free. Sometimes *I* don't know if I'm listening, or if it's just the echo of my own exhale.

# The God of Rattlesnakes

Here's a secret held by the sky: all that rattles is just a shaking skin;
a shimmy imitation of the wind through aspen. A sound born
somewhere between hollowness and bone, that lick-split circa-second
shared by vortices of hummingbird wings. Fear announces itself like
rainfall, gently eroding stone. In my name, it can fiddle into unfamiliar
forms, or slowly sidewind its way back into the ground.

# The God of Pteropods

When I crafted your delicate shell-body from the crystal lattice of aragonite, I was spellbound by the thought of *fly-swimming*; of a sea snail, flapping a wing-foot freely through ambiguous blue. I never envisioned your death by dissolution, that your ocean-sky might one day corrode you from the outside in. It's a blurred line between shell and self—who shelters who? Recover from the penultimate whorl. Take your wing-foot and out fly-run acid-base equilibria.

## The God of Monarchs

Front-runner for candidacy of the Republic's arthropod: H.J. Res. 411: *Designating the monarch butterfly as the national insect of the United States.* Subject areas: government operations and policies; emblems; insects. 34 cosponsors; dead on introduction. Ninety percent decline in two decades raises doubt . . . List "butterfly" as *threatened*, followed by "nation-state." An insect emblem that's irksome. Aposematism is fool's gold, a beckoning flag that arrests the heart.

*House Joint Resolution (H.J. Res) 411 was introduced into the 101st United States Congress in 1989 to designate the monarch butterfly as the national insect. It was referred to the Committee on Post Office and Civil Service but was not enacted.*

# The God of Vaquitas

Each individual is 3.3% of what's left of a nine-tenths devoured pie. Certainty is 100% a lost cause, yet the chant survives: *¡Viva la vaquita marina!* Lifelong swimmers drown in droves, strangled in shallows of a vermillion sea. To live long is to buoy the body with soul. We are haunted by names for a knowingness, to leave the last bite on the plate untouched. In English, we call it *manners-bit,* "for the sake of good manners." In Spanish, *la vergüenza*— "the shame."

## The God of Mozambique Elephants

It was an “aha” moment: largest land mammal with overgrown teeth. I fancied tusks as bona fide majesty, not as billiard balls or opium pipes. Tusklessness arose as an asylum. What is a handicap, anyhow? The ability to debark trees? To upwell water to gasping riverbeds? To caress our young? At night I lie awake and listen to the subsonic rumbles of your repartee, the tremor of *hallelujah* in every step.

## The God of Jellyfish

I didn't forget your spine. I just remembered water first. Then movement—a dancer at the Royal Ballet springing sous-sus, the undulation of tulle. I stopped there, transfixed, and left you to dance. They say watercolor is the most unforgiving medium—hard to control, harder to erase, easy to overdo. Creation is a bit like that. If you don't have a plan, better to quit while you're ahead. Better to let water move you than to move water. Better to view your own transparency as masterpiece. Paint backwards from light to dark. Become immortal and then bisect yourself—root down and let the other half float away.

# The God of Sandhill Cranes

From this bird's-eye view of a bird's back, your likeness to the crucifix in flight strikes like an open palm. Wingspan that could tap an elephant's shoulder while tickling leathered toes. Ten million-year-old fossil wins you the oldest bird in the world—nowadays unthreading heirloom quilts of corn, still belting those wild, rolling *rs*. So-called "ribeye of the sky," let me teach you how to die: in the rigidity of right angles, crimson forehead weeping like a crown of thorns.

# The God of Giant Palouse Earthworms

I read about you in the weekly, "a rare American original." Storied soil steward—*Lowly Earthworm Plays Big Role*. Number three of "10 Animals We Thought Were Extinct But Aren't." Two specimens unearthed in 2010, spewing lily-scented saliva. "Meet Subterranean Bigfoot." The stories stretch like your elastic annuli. Now you're "Moby Worm," a great white spineless whale. Aristotle plagiarized my mind when he conjured the coiled intestines of the earth.

## The God of Magpies

Like a poet, pilfer the beauty passed over. Pick your words and pocket them like tinsel: iridescence and reminiscence. Find rhyme in the phonebook. Cache paraphrases, slang salutations, bottle caps, abbreviations. *Hey-yo Heineken!* Inquisitiveness is next to Godliness. One nickel at a time, thou shalt steal from the sidewalk to pay back the soil.

## The God of Long-Footed Potoroos

/mär'sōōpēəl/. Admittedly, the word is fun to say—a Ferris wheel ride of inflections. Here, within the mammalian infraclass, the long-footed potoroo: another amusement for the mouth, and the largest of rat-kangaroos. You chatter in a chain of *kiss kiss, kiss kiss,* scattering the sporocarps of hypogeal fungi. Sometimes we speak in commandments when we should speak in song. Keep rooting fruiting fungi, potoroo. Take the tongue of the world and wring it like a wet towel.

# The God of Barn Owls

Learn to fly on the smooth oysters of westerlies, apart from our acoustical landscape. Antiphony is the harmony produced by oppositions of sound. Unlike yours—the consonance of an echo with no reply. In that silent plunge, the face of fog swoops down with its eyes scissored out of sheet, transposed with opposable talons—the motions of sound and body swallowed whole. The cantor's calls are answered only by quakings of rafters. The Japanese word *Ya* has no counterpart in English. The nearest equivalent is a semicolon, or "watch closely now before the trapeze artist falls."

# The God of Bull Trout

I'm in love with the word *adfluvial*, rhymes with *alluvial*—the former a life form, the latter a fan. Limnology moves through the mouth like cursive on pages, spills fluidly as fountain pens. Try *Salvelinus confluentus*. The tongue seduces the teeth, skips over *riffle and pool* like a polished stone. If only words furnished comfort like undercut banks. These days, clean streams fill the wanting space within compound nouns: *floodplain; oxbow; riprap*. Hide beside me under the hyphen of *log-jams*.

# The God of O'ahu Tree Snails

It's a ghost town in these treetops. Arboreal table for one. Fillet of fungus, medium-rare. Try out your eye stalks as chopsticks. What can I say? The snail days of summer don't turn pages. Embrace hermitage. Wind yourself into your own spiral cleavage. Malacology offers no Latin for loneliness. Bury your song in the earlobe of the leaf's surface. Sing until your voice becomes lore, and your tears dew.

## The God of Madrone Butterflies

I formed you to occupy the isolation of an entire genus. With a mountain range for a mother and the companionship of a leathery evergreen host plant, I dreamed you would find the nonstop consolation of solitude. Instead, you formed a sibling society of caterpillars, a lifetime lived as brother-sisters. You built shelter from spinning the silk of your mouth. You basked in your communal web-tent. You let in your kin and non-kin. I learned how to elevate my eyebrows. Surprise instills this insight: chew through solitude; find refuge in its venous skeleton.

# The God of Hainan Gibbons

They say if you boil your body into balm it promotes the downward movement of Qi. Which stifles hiccups. What's left is a total of thirteen torsos and twenty-six arms. Three grandfather-fathers, four daughter-mothers, three half-grandsons, two solitary males, one infant aunt-niece. Hardly a crowd, but hiccup-free. *Pendulus* means *hanging, uncertain*. The rebellious Qi flows to the liver, soothes the ache.

# The God of Saola

In 1992 the world discovered you in pieces. A species resurrected from bric-a-brac in hunters' houses: three sets of long, straight horns; two lower jaws; three complete hides salted and tacked to the wall. You were unknown to science, an enigma so enormous they published details of your cranium in *Nature*, alongside a photo of a stuffed skin.
*A new species of living bovid from Vietnam.*
Dental formula is 0 0 3 3 x 2 = 32,
3 1 3 3
with elongated premolars and incisors like pegs. They said you may "merit the creation of a new tribe." An invented genus in order Artiodactyla. Numbers around a hundred, or maybe ten. Are you still considered living if science hasn't seen you alive? I'm sure they'll recognize you by your skull, squint for dentitions in late occlusal wear.

# The God of Yangtze Finless Porpoises

This is how I learned fractions: from one thousand to eight hundred sixty-three is 13.7%. I felt your numbers fall, the thinning of porpoise pods. A percentage is a fraction, a splitting of a whole. It is a dimensionless number, and the loss too—a quantity missing a physical space. It's more like a feeling than a number. I felt your loss, river suckling, like the speed of light in a vacuum, like the constant pull of gravity. Keep grinning your spade-shaped teeth, your steep forehead unfurrowed. As your whistle fades, the muteness of water grows in unitless volume.

## The God of European Starlings

Your signal-to-noise ratio remains the fetal curl of a question mark. Sometimes it's a screeching seesaw, sometimes Mozart esteems. I didn't conceive of language, language conceived of me. Mimicry sires dialects from copycat sounds. Yodel your own call, songster, twined with car alarms. Triumphantly smack the spoken word as if to sweep the feet of Shakespeare. Repeat after me: sentences are slowly braking trains, off-key as Mozart's grief.

## The God of Arapaima

Of all the forms I've borne, this one blazes like gold. A mouthbreather who's also a mouthbrooder, with young on your tongue and lungs by your liver. Float this adage by your breath's apparatus: *Life's best lived at the interface, kissing the thin skin of surface tension . . .* Always smooch with your tongue teeth, slick and penetrant as bone. The principle of the soul is simple—that fish shouldn't drown. Yet here's the Amazon's trophy, sidelined and sucking wind.

## The God of Bison

I watched your bleached skulls pile up as high as a hawthorn tree.
Once, I shaped the soil around your cloven toes, and from your
hoofprint sprang the stubble of bluestem—my favorite five o'clock
shadow. "Ecologically extinct" means a tethered cloud, the wildness
worn out of you with cross-bred cattle. Signature shoulder hump
swapped for higher hind-quarters. More docile, they say; tender, but
with "hardihood intact." Timestamp the landscape with these hybrid
bones. Let rainwater refill the hollow of your relict wallows.

## The God of Centipedes

I gave not just with two hands but with one hundred. Or ninety-nine. I prefer to sculpt segments in odds. Don't worry about the schism between hands and feet, both can be joined in prayer. Immerse yourself into soil like a loam baptism. Hatch and devour your mother as sacrament-meal. If there is reincarnation, it's this: grow from your mother's fodder. Let your legs labor legs. Become a new, soft body. We grow by leaving our skeletons behind.

## The God of American Badgers

So lives a fury that could dig through stone. Claws that could crack asphalt, shape the soil matrix. Hollowed ground is your heirloom seed, passed through generations like a pocket watch. Time is in Einstein's mind, the reciprocal coordinate of space. And, here in the soil, thumbed through like chapters. Time is a gold pan for the lifespan, pores retaining only pollen grains and vacant space.

## The God of Devils Hole Pupfish

Whoever said a hole is not a home hasn't seen this limestone cavern: the verdure of diatom lawns grown lush on barn owl dung. Year-round, a balmy 92. *Peaceful micropolitan* doesn't do it justice. Privacy guaranteed by the noiseless neighbors of seven threatened plants. Waves splash walls only rarely. 2005: population of this Promised Land plunged to eighty-four, minus nine put on layaway in Mandalay Bay. Neon-blue scales now match signage of the Vegas strip. You and the Devil share these digs. It's got the Feng Shui of fluorescent gravel and the standing ovation of plastic pennywort.

# The God of Star-Nosed Moles

Let's replace our faces with a state of being. Wear intuition as an expression. Let ideas wrap a ring around the snout. Seeing is beyond light rays entering eyes. Here in the ground, vision is vestigial—redundant as *close proximity.* Let your senses wave like sea anemones. Make a wish on a fleck of mica. Move purposefully, somewhere between the speed of light and blinking.

# The God of Caddisfly Larvae

If animals owe nothing to art, then what are we to make of this hollow tube: a patchwork of the shapeliest stones, planorbid shells, and slivers of fish bones like spruce needles? Ethology is left hanging. Is it a work of art, an act of instinct, or an insect's artifact? Replace these sand grains with gold. Reconsider . . . Behold the oeuvre by hexapod hands, which can only be described as ruse.

*Inspired by the artwork of Hubert Duprat.*

## The God of Seahorses

If I had one piece of guidance for you, it would be this: *hold on to that Q-tip.* No, not to clean your coronet, or the lint between the twenty-six rings of your tail. Not to wipe clean the wax from the canals of your listening lateral line. Just grasp your tail around the plastic stem and sail. *Prehensile: adapted for seizing hold of something.* Hold anything. Remain anchored while adrift. Forget your toothlessness and suck in the sea. Swim circles around your lover. Hold fast.

*Inspired by Justin Hofman's photograph* "Sewage surfer."

# The God of Woodland Caribou

Today the last caribou left Idaho by life flight. Now, the snow of
the South Selkirk Mountains is engraved only by the tracks of
snowmobiles. Paired apostrophe toes ‘’ ‘’ ‘’ ‘’
replaced by phantom railroads ===== A thirty-year crusade ends in
this maternity pen, hoof-tromped trails hemmed by 12-foot walls. It
happened with a whimper. The deafening turn of rotor wings.

# The God of ʻAkikiki

I love all 468 of you, the small Kaua'i creeper, *Oreomystis bana.* The *'akikiki,* derived from *'akiki*—dwarfed, all twelve grams of you—the weight of two quarters; or sixty raindrops; four hundred grains of rice. All the ʻakikiki in the world weigh three-fifths of one Dachshund, a.k.a. not even one hot dog dog. I feel the weight of you like *a'a,* a full womb; *a'a'a*, a network of veins; *'ainā*, an assiduous ache. I cry out to you but *ua'ā'ā ka leo*—the reply is unintelligible. Islands raucously erupt, quietly erode. Keep calling, dwarfish bark-picker, until your muffled trill pricks the skin of our collective conscience.

# The God of Christmas Island Red Crabs

Molt by inhaling the sea and exhaling a speckle of atmosphere. Sea sucker turned air breather. To walk sideways is to *sidewalk*. A paved path for pedestrians, or my cooked-up verb for this red brick road tip-toeing back to the sea. Carmine waves close roads. *BABY CRABS RETURNING. WALKERS ONLY*. Sidewalk, side step, scuffle toe heel. Christmas decapods, out-dance those yellow crazy ants. Don't let your drum beat drown in that sixty million shuffle of invasive legs.

# The God of Eyelash Mites

The lash line's a nursery. A motherland of ecoparasites, a.k.a. face-feasters. Here's a face-off of factoids: 1. the face is the individual's most distinguishing feature, 2. the face is crowded as a farmer's market. A larva on every tenth lash crosses one earlobe length an hour. To conveners in the town square of dark circles, may you chase all your tears with sebum. Pave periorbital hardscapes.

## The God of Tardigrades

If I made you in my own image, it was before my morning coffee and concealer. You're cute in a certain light, moss piglet—maybe incandescent with eyelids closed. You're a slow stepper but a long stander. Five mass extinctions and some half billion years can't rob the chunk from all eight of your micro-thighs. Sometimes curling into a cryptobiotic fetal position is the precise response to a supernova. In the face of boiling oceans, order a catnap. Sometimes the solution is the snooze button. In the vacuum of space, let your stumpy legs applaud.

## The God of Narwhals

From my pelagic womb, I birthed an untamable beast with a horn protruding between its lashless eyes. You were a *monoceros*, until Latin surfaced its own name for your solitary tusk: a *unicornis*. A toothpick fit for the universe's sandwich. Skewer the ocean. The world is your sea kabob. Hide your mythos in the shrinking shadow of drift ice. Traverse the whole earth without ever touching the ground.

## The God of Pikas

Haying behavior is a chronic tic. 12,000 trips for eight months of food. A straw mountain is a meadow's half-eaten headstone. A straw man is an inflated opponent, like *carbon dioxide is not a pollutant* (an emissions omission). What's the weather down there? I heard you couldn't last an hour past 78°, whistle hare. Half sunny with a chance of oblivion. Mountaintops are eroding islands. Quick, climb these ladder rungs of tumbledown scree. Grab a seat in the sky. Watch your straw mountains become balloons, floating away with disbelief's buoyancy.

# The God of Surinam Toads

*Pipa* is a Portuguese kite and a frog with a back that is meant to be broken. Toes like a natal star, dorsal skin with the pits of pumice stone. Vesicular is the texture of gas fizzing from magma, or toadlings seething from the spine like springing crocuses. Seduce through the snapping of hyoid bones. Bear your eggs like goosebumps, like an unfamiliar skin. Be one hundred and one bodies and then just be one. This is the sensation of motherhood: holding on to slipping strings, flying while heavier than air.

# The God of Beavers

In my image, I made you a mover. A shaker of landscapes. A fellow ecosmith. Together we are groundshapers. *Semiaquatic rodent with buck teeth* was a postscript, to stymie rivalry in its infancy . . . Envy looks no lovelier on me. I know—it's easy to let business gnaw at you. Gnaw back until you've built breathlessness. Pause. Satiate your appetite with aspen cambium. Tinker with earthen sticks and spools. Cover the scaffold in mud. Now lie down in the construct and close your transparent eyelids.

## The God of Coconut Octopuses

I'm setting the record straight: the plural is octopuses, and coconuts are not a nut but a fibrous drupe. A drupe is a stone fruit in the genus *Prunus*, like an olive or apricot, except when a stone fruit is, in fact, an octopus. A tool is an instrument held in the hand. Or in this case, a muscular hydrostat. Stilt walk the seafloor in the stolen husk of a not-nut. Hold your own portable fortress. We measure intelligence by the manipulation of objects—to open a jar and dissolve in it. Illusion is an atrophied muscle. Unfurl. Let your brain escape into the nebulous space of the body.

# The God of Cougars

Cat of the mountain with a range that spans languages, weaving through the landscape like a braided stream. Total range: 8.1 million square miles. A home that's one-tenth of the world. IUCN Red List Status: *least concern*. Current population trend: *decreasing*. The world's urban growth is "quadratic-hyperbolic," the handle end of a hockey stick. Desert basins abut border walls and backyard pools. The neck is the body's most evocative shaft. Now aim for the nape. Leave only straight lines.

# The God of Chinese Giant Salamanders

Thirty-four contestants for *definition of a species* breeds taxonomic anarchy. Even Darwin—frontal lobes steeped in systematics like tea leaves—deemed defining a species undefinable. Here's the posterchild: *Andrias davidianus.* Shrouded river-lounger long as a queen-size bed, not one, but five wild clades. Cryptic lineages signal extinctions of fellow could-be species. Efficiency's axe fells five limbs with one swing. Both you and me, fruiting spurs on this shriveling tree.

## The God of Yellow-billed Cuckoos

Rarely-seen rain crow beckons the sky, begs nimbostratus: *ka ka ka ka ka kow kow kow!* Clouds spill themselves like stories to the ground. A *distinct population segment* is a theorem—not self-evident but proven by reasoned chains. *Distinctness* is the sum of discreteness and significance, somehow totals out to this body built by caterpillars and katydids. Of a two-ounce frame, one-half is feathers. The converse is this weighty newfound word—*zygodactyl*, a tongue-twister for your toehold. An adjective better suited to a verb: *to be gripped by both hindsight and foresight.*

# The God of Raccoons

Take up everything in your hands. Reflect on phalanges—*flex, extend, abduct, adduct, and circumduct.* In plantigrade movement, metatarsals greet ground. Listen closely to the peristalsis of earthworms. Watch light bend like limbs through water. Construct churches in crawlspaces, tree cavities, abandoned cars. Invite your fission-fusion family. Say grace over cat food. *C'est la vie.*

## The God of Humans

To love thy neighbor as thyself is the saintliest spadework. To worship the balance of wire-walking fox squirrels. To kneel beside Japanese beetle larvae curled like commas under the lawn. Let the sweat rain off your elbows! To regard the black-capped chickadee, bleached eggs like baby teeth. Now onto the starlings: egg evictors with planetarium plumage and song like a rusted bike chain. Life is an unperfected practice. If only *to live and let live* came as easy as *to walk and chew gum*. If only the mind were as worn as the mouth, a heart with the mileage of a crushed car cube. From this omnipotent angle, the world turns both clockwise and counter-. Life is born in Brownian motion and bound in amber. Sometimes I stare at the sun until the Earth is just another shadow afloat my vitreous fluid.

# Notes

Some of the poems in this collection quote from the following articles:

Barker, R. (2019, March 1). "What extinction in Idaho looks like: Last caribou captured, ending conservation program." *The Idaho Statesman*. (The God of Woodland Caribou)

Gilmore, N. (2018, May 18). "10 U.S. species that aren't extinct anymore." *The Saturday Evening Post*. (The God of Giant Palouse Earthworms)

Montgomery, S. (2016, October 16). "Meet the giant Palouse earthworm, a rare American original." *The Boston Globe*. (The God of Giant Palouse Earthworms)

Van Dung, V., Giao, P. M., Chinh, N. N., Tuoc, D., Arctander, P., & MacKinnon, J. (1993). A new species of living bovid from Vietnam. *Nature*, 363(6428), 443-445. (The God of Saola)

Weaver, M. (2016, November 25). "Lowly earthworm plays big role." *Capital Press*. (The God of Giant Palouse Earthworms)

Other poems were inspired by the following articles and artwork:

Blankenbuehler, P. (2019, April 15). "How a tiny endangered species put a man in prison." *High Country News*. (The God of Desert Hole Pupfish)

Dearing, M. D. (1997). The function of haypiles of pikas *(Ochotona princeps). Journal of Mammalogy, 78*(4), 1156-1163. (The God of Pikas)

Duprat, H., Besson, C., & Pleasance, S. (1998). The wonderful caddis worm: Sculptural work in collaboration with Trichoptera. *Leonardo, 31*(3), 173-177. (The God of Caddisfly larvae)

Duprat, H. "Caddis worms building their case," 1980-2015. Galerie Art: Concept, Paris. (The God of Caddisfly larvae)

Hofman, J. "Sewage surfer." Natural History Museum, London. (The God of Seahorses)

Jacobs, J. (2019, January 10) "George the Snail, Believed to Be the Last of His Species, Dies at 14 in Hawaii." *The New York Times.* (The God of The God of O'ahu Tree Snails)

Kahn, J. (2018, March 14). "Should some species be allowed to die out?" *New York Times Magazine.* (The God of the 'Akikiki)

Maron, Dina F. (2018, November 9). "Under poaching pressure, elephants are evolving to lose their tusks." *National Geographic.* (The God of Mozambique Elephants)

Pennisi, E. (2017, December 7). "Melting sea ice is stressing out narwhals." Science Magazine. doi:10.1126/science.aar6991 (The God of Narwhals)

White, N. (2018, January 10). "March of the red crabs." *Daily Mail Australia.* (The God of Christmas Island Red Crabs)

## Acknowledgements

I thank the editors of the following journals for first publishing these poems, some of them in slightly different forms:

*Animal: A Beast of a Literary Magazine:* "The God of Eyelash Mites," "The God of Tardigrades," "The God of Centipedes"
*Arkana Magazine:* "The God of Caddisfly larvae," "The God of Star-Nosed Moles"
*The Curlew:* "The God of Racoons," "The God of Magpies," "The God of Jellyfish," "The God of Madrone Butterflies," "The God of Star-Nosed Moles"
*The Ecological Citizen:* "The God of Pikas," "The God of Surinam Toads," "The God of Chinese Giant Salamanders," "The God of Vaquitas," "The God of Saola"
*Flyway: Journal of Writing & Environment:* "The God of Olms," "The God of Coconut Octopuses," "The God of Mozambique Elephants"
*Postcard Poems and Prose:* "The God of Rattlesnakes"
*Saltfront: studies in human habit(at):* "The God of Bull Trout"
*Take a Stand,* A Raven Chronicles Press Anthology: "The God of Monarchs," "The God of Vaquitas"

And thanks to my editor, Rachel Nolan, for fine-tuning the final forms.